W9-AQB-090

DEC 1 2000

J
612.82
FUR

Furgang, Kathy.
My brain

WITHDRAWN

WARRENVILLE PUBLIC LIBRARY DISTRICT
28W751 Stafford Place
Warrenville, IL 60555

My Brain

Kathy Furgang

WARRENVILLE PUBLIC LIBRARY
28W751 STAFFORD PLACE
WARRENVILLE, IL 60555

The Rosen Publishing Group's
PowerKids Press™
New York

For Adam

Published in 2001 by The Rosen Publishing Group, Inc.
29 East 21st Street, New York, NY 10010

Copyright © 2001 by The Rosen Publishing Group, Inc.

All rights reserved. No part of this book may be reproduced in any form without permission in writing from the publisher, except by a reviewer.

First Edition

Book Design: Kim Sonsky

Illustration Credits: All organ 3-D illustrations © LifeArt/TechPool Studios, Inc; All other 3-D illustrations by Kim Sonsky.
Photo Credits: Pp. 7, 20 © Photo Resource; p. 19 © Gazelle Technologies, Inc.

Furgang, Kathy.
    My brain / Kathy Furgang.—1st ed.
        p. cm. — (My body)
    Includes index.
    Summary: Describes the different parts of the brain and how they function.
    ISBN 0-8239-5571-0 (lib bdg.)
    1. Brain—Juvenile literature. 2. Neurophysiology—Juvenile literature. [1 Brain.] I. Title

    QP361.5F87 2001
    612.8'2—dc21   99-053834

Manufactured in the United States of America

ROSEN 10/25/00
14.50

Contents

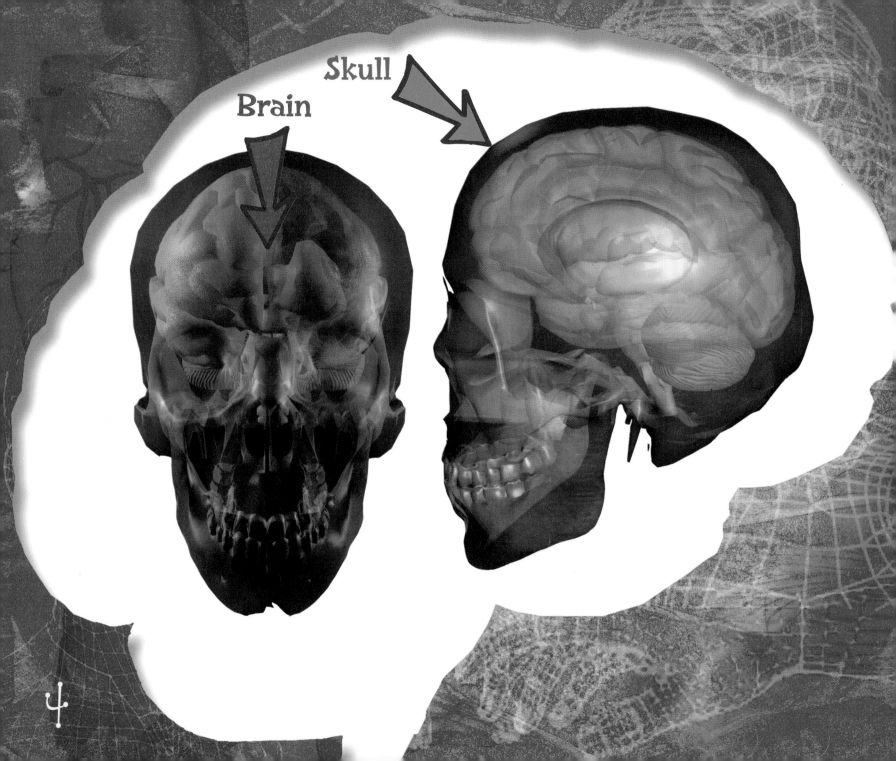

Brain

Skull

4

Your Busy Brain

Your brain is the most important part of your body. Think of everything you do during the day. You walk, talk, eat, laugh, play games, learn, and sleep. You are able to do these things because of your brain. Your brain is a message center that tells the rest of your body what to do. Thousands of messages are sent to and from your brain every second. Your brain is always working. It is a soft, wrinkled, and pinkish gray body part. The brain is kept safe inside your head by the hardest bone in your body, the skull.

This is what your brain looks like inside your skull. A full-grown human brain weighs three pounds. It is almost full size by the age of five.

Talking to Your Body

There is a book on the table. Your eyes send a message to your brain. Your brain sends a message to your arm and hand to pick up the book. How does your brain talk to the rest of your body? Tiny fibers called **nerves** quickly carry information from the brain to places around the body. Messages travel up and down along the **spinal cord**. The spinal cord is a long row of nerves that run down your back. The messages then go to areas all over your body. The brain and the spinal cord together are called the **central nervous system**.

In the time it takes you to read these words, your brain has sent thousands of messages around your body and you didn't even feel it!

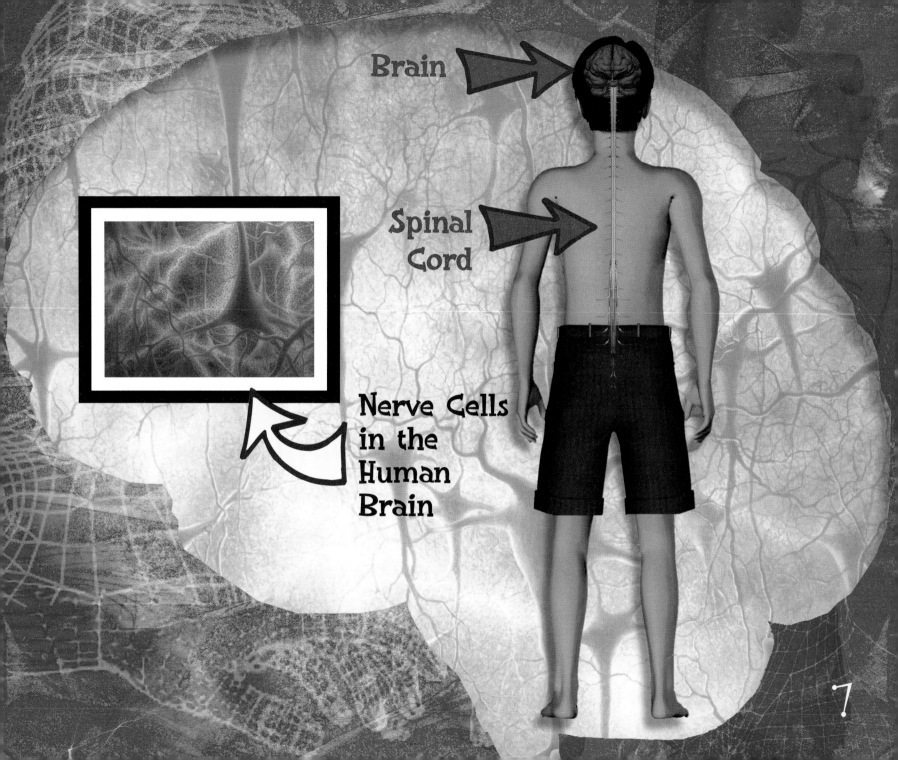

Brain

Spinal
Cord

Nerve Cells
in the
Human
Brain

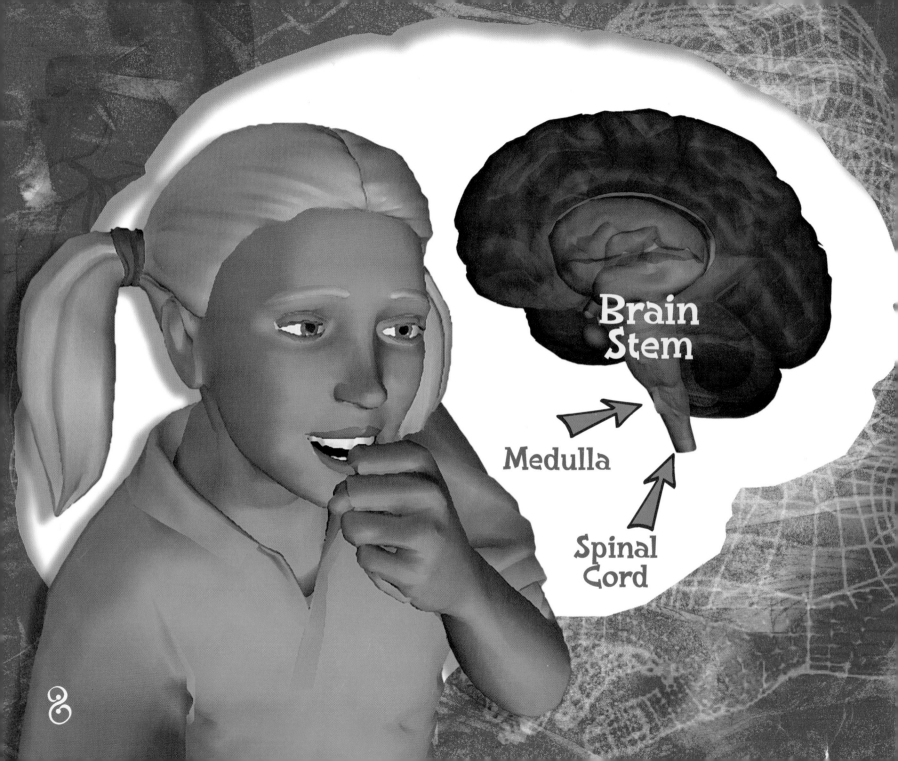

Your Brain Stem

The bottom part of your brain near your spinal cord is called the **brain stem**. It helps your body do the things that you don't even think about. When you blink, swallow, cough, or feel pain, a part of your brain stem called the **medulla** is sending the messages. It keeps you breathing, your heart beating, and your eyes blinking. Your brain stem also helps you to stay safe. When you touch something hot, it sends a quick message for you to move your hand away from the heat.

Your brain sends the message so fast that you don't even have time to think about it. This is called a **reflex**.

You have a lot to think about every day. Your brain stem takes care of certain things for you, such as coughing, so you don't have to think about them.

Happy Face or Sad Face?

Our **emotions** come from the top part of our brain stem. Emotions are feelings like being happy, sad, excited, or angry. Sometimes a friend makes you happy. Sometimes you are scared of something. Messages about how you feel come from your brain stem. The **hypothalamus** is the part of your brain that lets you have different kinds of emotions. The different parts of your brain are always talking to each other. One part of your brain tells you how you feel. Another part tells you what to think and do about it.

Poets say that we feel emotions with our hearts. Scientists have shown, though, that feelings and emotions come from our brains.

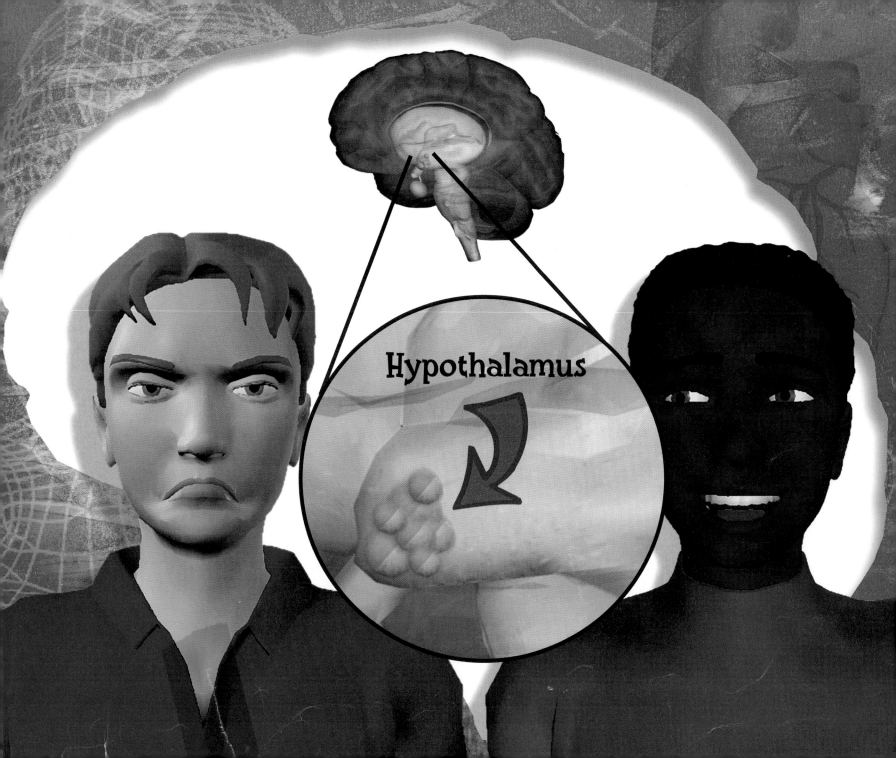

Hypothalamus

Cerebellum

WARRENVILLE PUBLIC LIBRARY DISTRICT

Smooth Moves

When you kick a soccer ball or walk up stairs, the part of your brain called the **cerebellum** is hard at work. The cerebellum allows you to move your body and balance yourself. The combination of good balance and smooth body movements is called **coordination**. Your cerebellum is right above your brain stem. It is about the size of an apple and it is filled with tiny folds, or wrinkles. When you want to move, strong nerve cells quickly travel throughout your body to tell you what to do. Your eyes send a message back to your brain about when and where to move your leg to kick the soccer ball. Your brain works together with your body to help it move.

Millions of nerve cells are at work when you do a trick like turning a handstand into a backbend.

A Computer in Your Head

The largest part of your brain is called the **cerebrum**. It is soft, pinkish gray, and wrinkled. The outer part of your cerebrum is called the **cortex**. This is the part of your brain that lets you think about things and learn. It also allows you to remember things. Like a computer, the cerebrum stores facts and information that you have learned. The cerebrum also controls your **senses**. Messages about taste, smell, touch, hearing, and sight are all sent to different parts of your cerebrum. Humans are the smartest animals on Earth. We are the only animal that can learn about what our brain does.

The cerebrum makes up about 85 percent of the brain's weight. The cortex is involved in many brain functions, including sight, speech, hearing, and memory.

Cerebrum

Cortex

15

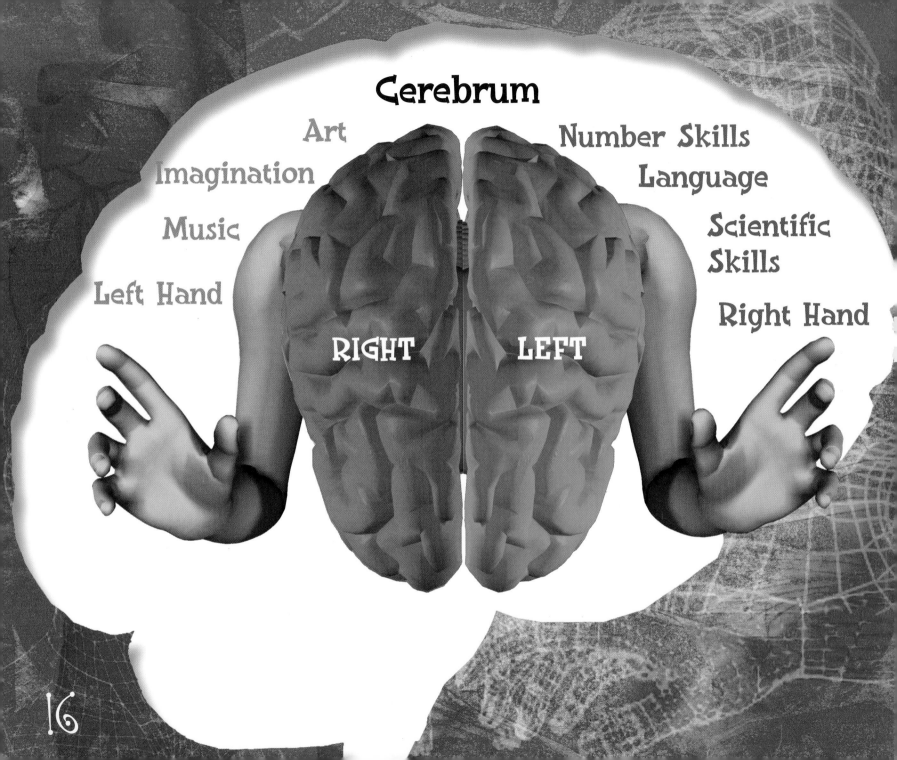

Left Brain, Right Brain

The cerebrum is made of two halves. The right half and the left half are split down the middle. Nerve cells connect the two halves to each other. Nerve cells shoot messages back and forth between the two parts. One side always knows what the other side is doing. Scientists have found that the right half of your brain controls the left half of your body. The left half of your brain controls the right half of your body. Raise your right hand. It was the left half of your brain that helped you to do it.

Are you right-handed or left-handed? Most people use one side of their body more than the other. That means they use one side of their brain more than the other.

17

A Map of Your Brain

People who are good at art use the right side of their brain the most. The left side of our brain is the part that helps us with math. Scientists have found that different parts of your brain help you with different things such as sight, movement, and speech. The control center for music is on the right side of your brain. Messages about reading and writing come from the left side. Most things we do, however, use both sides of our brain.

Most of the things you do use both sides of your brain. When playing video games, your right brain sees the screen and your left brain decides on the next move.

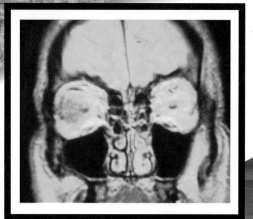

In a CAT scan, an image is made by computerized tomography. This means that X rays are used to take a picture of the brain.

Movements

Emotion and Memory

Vision

Senses

Balance

19

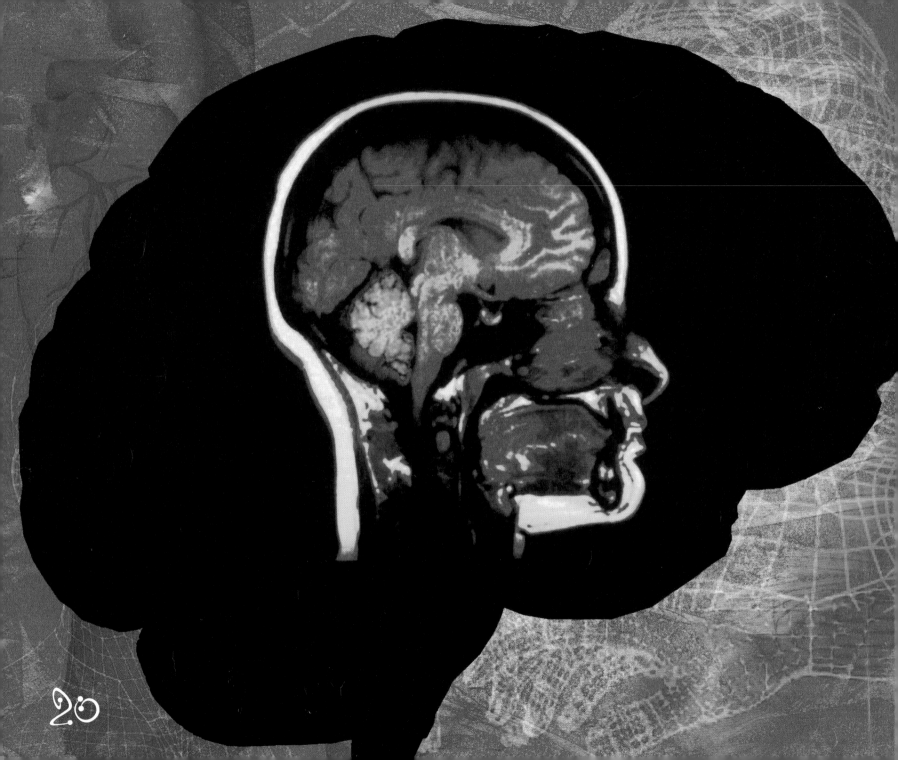

Brain Trouble

Sometimes nerve cells do not always send the right messages. This causes our brains to get mixed up. When our brains do not work right, it is called a disorder. When blood cannot go to a certain part of the brain, it is called a stroke. Many people who have had strokes cannot move one side of their body.

Other brain problems can involve memory. We have millions of brain cells. It is natural for brain cells to die off slowly as we grow old. That is why many older people sometimes have problems remembering things.

In magnetic resonance imaging (MRI), radio waves are used in a highly magnetic field to take a picture of the brain. This is an MRI of a 66-year-old man.

How Do We Know About the Brain?

It has taken scientists a long time to learn about the brain. There is still a lot that we do not know. Doctors have learned a lot from people who have had brain disorders or who have been hurt. They have learned how damage to our brain affects the rest of our body. Since the 1960s, there have been ways to take special pictures of the brain. The pictures may tell what part of someone's brain has a problem. In the years to come, scientists may learn a lot more about our brains, how they work, and how to correct problems that happen in the brain.

Glossary

brain stem (BRAYN STEM) The bottom part of the brain near the spinal cord.

central nervous system (SEN-trul NUR-vus SIS-tim) The brain and the spinal cord together.

cerebellum (ser-eh-BEL-um) A part of the brain found in the back of the skull that helps with balance and movement.

cerebrum (ser-EE-brem) The largest part of the brain. It allows animals to think and remember things and store facts and knowledge.

coordination (koh-OR-dih-nay-shun) Balance and smooth movement of the body.

cortex (KOR-tex) The outer layer of your cerebrum that is pinkish gray and wrinkled.

emotions (ee-MOH-shunz) Strong feelings such as anger or sadness.

hypothalamus (hy-poh-THAL-uh-mus) The part of the brain that controls emotions.

medulla (meh-DOO-la) The part of the brain stem that controls the body's basic functions, such as breathing, blinking, and sneezing.

nerves (NURVZ) Tiny fibers that carry information from the brain to places all around the body.

reflex (REE-fleks) An automatic response to something.

senses (SEN-sez) Taste, smell, touch, hearing, and sight.

spinal cord (SPY-nil KORD) A long row of nerve cells that go down the back.

23

Index

B
body, 5, 6, 13
brain stem, 9, 10, 13

C
central nervous system, 6
cerebellum, 13
cerebrum, 14, 17
coordination, 13
cortex, 14

D
disorder, 21, 22

H
hypothalamus, 10

M
medulla, 9

N
nerves, 6, 13, 17, 21

R
reflex, 9

S
scientists, 17, 18, 22
senses, 14
skull, 5
spinal cord, 6, 9

Web Sites

To find out more about the brain, check out these Web sites:
http://faculty.washington.edu/chudler/colorbook.html
http://tqjunior.advanced.org/5777/ner2.htm
http://tqjunior.advanced.org/5777/ner3.htm